Mediation

Preparation

How to Prepare for Mediation

by Joe B. Hewitt

A Guide for Anyone Going Into Mediation

Mediation Preparation
By Joe B. Hewitt
Copyright 2015, Joe B. Hewitt
ISBN- 13: 978-1514863763
ISBN-10: 1514863766

Table of Contents

Mediation Preparation
By Joe B. Hewitt
Copyright 2015, Joe B. Hewitt
ISBN- 13: 978-1514863763
ISBN-10: 1514863766

Acknowledgements

Thanks to my wife, Marona Posey's examination of my manuscript through her eyes as an attorney and published author. Thanks to the Hon. Dale B. Tillery, Judge, 134th District Court, Dallas, Texas, for reading the manuscript and endorsing the book. Thanks to literary critics and dear friends Jim Hazelip and Nancy Riddick for honest, constructive criticism of the manuscript.

Prologue

Medi-a-tion or Medi-ta-tion

A little "t" between friends makes a big difference.
A meditator thinks about thinking and doesn't have to do anything else. Usually no one else is involved in his meditation. A person meditating on the Word of God would be quietly thinking of what the Bible teaches.

Meditators can meditate about any number of things or nothing at all. He/she may meditate about a mental journey into nothingness that the Eastern religions call nirvana, a state in which you cease to think. Most other people would consider it being dead.

A mediator stands between two people in conflict and helps them settle their differences. The Mediator is a go-between, sometimes called a neutral third party. Like the referee in a boxing match, the Mediator is in charge of the proceedings and makes sure the rules of courtesy are followed and that no person abuses another. Unlike a court trial where the judge decides who's right and who's wrong, the Mediator makes no judgment. Rather, the Mediator helps both parties equally to arrive at a settlement agreement that both parties can live with.

Mediation is sometimes confused with arbitration. An arbitrator is more like a judge who decides who is right and who is wrong and who pays whom. The Mediator makes no such decisions but rather helps both parties to arrive at a settlement agreement.

Mediation Preparation

By Joe B. Hewitt
Copyright 2015, Joe B. Hewitt

The purpose of this is to help both attorneys and laymen get ready to participate in mediation. It is not intended to give legal advice.

Some Unusual Cases *A Composite*

While I am careful to not break the confidentiality rules, here is a mediation session that is not at all typical. Rather, it has elements of several strange cases put together. Identities are fictitious.

I sat at the end of a long conference table. A file folder lay on the table in front of me. The folder' jacket has the words, "Hewitt and Hewitt Mediators, DC-10-1314, Smith vs Jones. Below that are names of attorneys and contact information. Below that the lined sheet has a handwritten note of each correspondence, email message, and phone call made to the attorneys.

The Plaintiff, Mr. Alexander Smith, a tall slender man in his early 40s with a short sparse blond beard, arrived first. "My attorney is on his way," he said.

"I'm Joe Hewitt," said I, extending my hand. We shook hands and I invited Mr. Smith to sit at my left.

"Ah, here he is now," Alexander Smith said. He introduced his attorney, Paul Prichard, to the group. Prichard, a small young man was dressed informally in a black silk shirt, gray pants and gray Italian shoes with soles so thin they looked uncomfortable. He repeated each person's name in a deep bass voice.

The Defendant, Stephen Jones, a nervous polite guy in his early 50s wearing a white baseball cap came in with his attorney, Darrell Dickins, shorter than the other two men and dressed as if for court, in a dark navy blue suit with a patterned light blue tie. I invited them to sit at my right.

After explaining where to find drinks and location of restrooms, I asked the parties, "Have you been in mediation before?"

Neither Alexander Smith nor Stephen Jones had been in mediation before, so I explained:

"Mediation is for the benefit of all concerned, the Plaintiff, the Defendant, and the Court. If we can settle this case in mediation, it will save everyone time, trouble and money.

"Well, I'm for that," the Plaintiff, Mr. Smith said.

I continued, "Some 90 % of civil cases filed in large cities such as Dallas never go to trial but are settled beforehand by the attorneys or in mediation. If it were not for mediation we wouldn't have enough courthouses or judges to handle the load.

"Over all, 80 % of cases that go to mediation are settled. Some of us have much better rates of settlement than that, but 80 % isn't bad. Before I continue, there is an important order of business we need to take care of. Did you bring a check?"

Each attorney slid a check across to me. I put the checks in the file folder, "Thank you. Now to continue:

"This is not a trial. I am not a judge. This is an informal meeting without strict procedural rules. I prefer that we continue on a first name basis. I'm Joe. Is that okay with you?"

"Sure," The Plaintiff, Alexander Smith said. "I'm Alexander."

The others spoke up, giving their first names, "I'm Paul. . ." *That deep voice should qualify him for a spot in a barbershop quartet singing group*, I thought.

"I'm Steve. . ." The Defendant pushed the bill of his cap up with a finger.

"I'm Darrell, but this is all a waste of time. The only reason we're here is because the Court ordered us to be here." The dapper attorney Darrell stood. "Now we have appeared. We have paid. We have complied with the Court order, now we are leaving." He shoved papers into a black leather briefcase.

Keeping my voice on an even keel, I said, "Darrell, you know the rules as well as I do. I am not in charge of the results of this mediation, you, the parties are. But I am in charge of the process. Mediation is not concluded until I determine that it is. In just a few minutes we will divide up, and I will be glad to listen to your concerns at that time."

"Well, it's no use. It's a waste of time," Darrell said, and sat back down.

"Now, let's continue with the explanation of mediation to the parties who have not experienced it," I said, and continued. "Everything that is said and done in the mediation session is confidential. Nothing that is discovered here can be used in court later if we do not reach a settlement and have to go to trial. The only exceptions are child abuse or elder abuse. Texas law requires us to report those.

"First, I will ask the Plaintiff to explain his position, then the Defense. I will try to understand each side's position.

"After we have explored options for settlement, and hopefully have reached a settlement, I will ask one of the attorneys to write up the agreement. After all have signed, I will take it upstairs and make copies for everyone. Each will have a copy of the handwritten, binding agreement. One of the attorneys will draw up the final document, which all will sign. And that's it; no trial It's all over.

"Now, Paul, are you ready to make your presentation?"

"Yes," Paul continued. "It's a simple breach of contract case. Alexander bought a dog from Steve. Steve refused to give him the registration papers for the dog, greatly diminishing its value." Paul gestured with both hands and revealed manicured fingernails painted with a clear polish.

About that time the door opened and a tall red-haired attractive woman dressed in a dark green business suit came in. I caught a whiff of a floral perfume.

"This is my wife, Penelope, Alexander said.

She acknowledged the others at the table and sat by her husband. She mumbled close to his ear. "Damn. I wish you hadn't done this."

Alexander ignored his wife's remark, stood and reached across the table, shaking a finger toward Steve. "You're the liar. You sold that dog and welched on the deal."

Steve jumped to his feet. "That's a lie. I didn't sell that dog. I loaned him to you for stud service. You stole my dog."

I interrupted the shouting match. "Ordinarily at that point I will ask for suggestions for settlement, but in this case, perhaps we should go ahead and divide up, leaving one party here, and taking the other party to the break-out room."

I stood, picked up my file folder, and asked Darrell, "Would you and Steve come with me?" As I watched the obviously high-priced lawyer in his Brooks Brothers suit and his client in a baseball cap, blue jeans and a t-shirt, I decided they were at least on the surface quite unlike one another. This is not unusual in attorneys and clients who work together in mediation.

I led them into a smaller room and shut the heavy door that prevented any sound from passing from one party to the other. One wall of the small room was covered with windows with a view of the parking lot. I had placed a bowl of hard candy and some small packages of snacks in the center of the small table, which lent the only color to the room. I sat across from Darrell and Steve. "Now, what would you like to see done here today?

Steve spoke up, "I want my dog back, and all the puppies he sired, and I want $20,000 to make up for what Alexander's keeping Pepe for the past two years cost me."

Darrell added, "Don't forget attorneys' fees and legal costs. It's a breach of contract, so you need to add another $7,000 to that."

I said, "Alexander is suing you for breach of contract. Have you counter-sued?"

"No, not yet. But I will, as soon as I leave this place," Darrell said.

"Okay. So you are demanding what? What's the bottom line?"

"Well, the puppies are probably far away now, so he needs to pay me for them. Pepe is a champion, and he sires champions. His puppies, especially the little teacup size male Chihuahuas, are worth a fortune. I'd say, give me back my Pepe, and $50,000 and I'll be satisfied."

"I told you it was a waste of time, "Darrell said, and reached into the candy dish for a mint." We will go to trial and prevail."

(Ordinarily I spend time first with the Plaintiff in caucus, but in this case with volatile Darrell, I dealt with him first.)

I excused myself and went back to the main conference room with its long table flanked by a dozen high-back swivel, leather covered chairs, and lighted by multi-colored lights hanging over the table. In addition to the colorful

lights, one wall was covered with modern, abstract paintings.
I hoped Steve and Darrell in the drab room didn't resent being placed there.

Seated at the head of the long conference table with Paul, Alexander and Penelope, I asked, "What would you like to see done here today?"

"I want Steve off my back and I want damages and attorney fees for his breach of contract," Alexander said.

"Do you have a bottom line?"

"Yes, I figure he has cost me at least $20,000 because he sold me a breeding male Chihuahua, and refused to give me the registration papers," Alexander said. "A champion Chihuahua is not worth much without papers."

"Is that the bottom line?"

"No. I'm out another $3,000 in attorney fees, and another $2,500 in veterinary fees. It amounts to $25,500. If he'll give me a check for that amount today, and the papers on Pepe, the dog, I'll be satisfied," Alexander said.

"May I see the contract?" I asked.

"Ha, ha, ha," Penelope chided.

"Well, we didn't put it in writing, but we have an oral contract," Alexander said.

"What do you suppose that contract is worth?" Penelope asked. ". . . the paper it's not written on?"

"It's still a contract," Paul said. "Steve agreed to sell Pepe for $9,000. Alexander gave Steve a check for that amount and took Pepe home with him. Steve said he would get the registration papers out of his safe deposit box the following day and deliver them to Alexander. That was the contract."

"So, how was it breached?" I asked.

"Steve didn't show up the next day with the registration papers. I called. He wouldn't return my calls," Alexander said. "I called a dozen times. Once a lady who cleans their house answered the phone. She said that Steve's wife had gone to Fort Worth to stay with her sister and Steve was out with a client.

Paul said, "Steve was nowhere to be found. Then a week later Steve showed up at Alexander's home demanding that he return Pepe to Steve and pay Steve a stud fee."

"My wife Penelope was scared to death of Steve," Alexander said. "Steve was stomping around in my house, shouting, 'Where's my dog?' I told him that I had paid him $9,000 and that he either should give me a refund or registration papers for the dog." Penelope grabbed Pepe and went out into the kennels to hide. I had to forcibly push Steve out of my house."

"What about the $9,000?" I asked.

"The check was never cashed. Steve denied ever receiving it. He claimed he loaned Pepe for stud service, and that was all. He accused us of stealing his dog," Alexander said.

I withdrew a form from the file folder that had printed above two columns of lines, Plaintiff's Demand and Defendant's Response. I had already written the Defendant's demand of "Return of the dog, Pepe, and $50,000."

Under Plaintiff's Demand, I wrote, "Alexander wants registration papers plus $25,000."

"I want to be clear on what you are demanding to settle this case," I said. "You want Pepe's registration papers and $25,000 cash to settle the case. Is that correct?"

"Yes. That is correct," Alexander and Paul both spoke up.

I excused myself and trudged back to the smaller room with my optimism dragging the floor.

Steve sat leaned back in the cushioned chair, rested his feet on a fold-up chair, and covered his eyes with a white baseball cap emblazoned with a big red "T."

I resumed my seat, laid the file folder on the small table and conveyed the Plaintiff's demand.

Steve jerked the white baseball cap off his head, sat up straight, and said gruffly, "What a liar."

"Had you done business with Alexander prior to this?" I asked.

"Yes," Steve said.

"Did you have problems with him before?" I asked.

"No. I did lots of business with Alexander," Steve said. "He always proved to be a man of his word. I don't know what's come over him."

"Was there a period of negotiation before the alleged transaction involving Pepe?" I asked.

"Yes. Ever since Pepe sired his first litter of puppies that turned out so small, Alexander wanted him. You see, these little teacup Chihuahua females can't have puppies. They're too small, but they do bring good prices as pets. If they do breed, the puppies are few in number, and don't live. So the female has to be a good sized, purebred Chihuahua, but the sire has to be as tiny as possible," Steve said.

"We bargained back and forth for several weeks, and finally agreed on $9,000. Alexander got the dog, but I never got the money. Apparently he changed his mind about buying the dog. However, since he had the dog in his possession, he owed me stud fees."

Darrell spoke up. "Steve was cheated out of a valuable dog. He should get the dog back plus stud fees plus the value of any puppies sired while in Alexander's possession. Steve is the victim here. Any judge or jury would agree. Alexander needs to deliver all these demands."

***

I went back into the large conference room where Alexander and Penelope were having a quiet spat that Paul appeared to ignore.

"Tell me about the deal to sell Pepe," I said.

"We agreed on a sale price of $9,000," Alexander said. "It was on a Saturday. He gave me Pepe and told me he would get the necessary registration papers out of his safe deposit box on Monday, and I would give him a check. On Monday he stayed out of reach. And a week later he denied the sale and claimed he just loaned Pepe out for stud service."

I laid out several scenarios: "What if you simply returned the dog? Apparently Steve never received payment."

"Absolutely not," both Paul and Alexander said. I tried several other "what-ifs," each of which was met with negative scorn.

After several minutes of hearing my suggestions shot down, I started back to the other room.

***

As I made my way back to the small room, a voice from 13 years ago returned in my memory, "Questions. Keep asking questions," Dr. Nancy Ferrell had repeated during a mediation training session.

In the small room I found Darrell busily tapping out keys on his laptop computer, obviously taking care of other business while he waited.

"So, what did they say?" Steve asked.

"No surprise," I answered.

"No deal. That's no surprise," Steve said.

"Alexander tells me that there were several weeks of negotiation before the alleged sale of Pepe," I said.

"Yes, several weeks. But when we finally arrived at a price, Alexander took the dog and never paid for him.

Failing to get Steve to change his demands, I went back to the large conference room.

> *Note: A Mediator spends lots of time going back and forth from one conference room to the other. On rare occasions he will keep both parties together in the same conference room throughout the entire mediation session. However, most of the time having the parties in separate rooms is better. They can speak more frankly, and convey only well-thought-out suggestions for settlement to the other side.*

***

Back in the large conference room, Alexander and Penelope were again of different opinions.

"I've had enough of this. I'm going home, Penelope said.

"You're involved in this. You need to stay," Alexander said.

"You need to stay," Paul said, looking up from his computer.

"In previous years, dealing with Steve, did he prove to be a man of his word?" I asked.

"That was then. This is now," Paul said.

"Did you trust Steve?" I asked

"No," Penelope said emphatically.

"I did back then," Alexander said.

"So earlier, he was a man of his word; is that right?" I asked.

"Yes, up until this incident," Alexander said.

"Tell me about the $9,000. Did you pay it?" I asked.

"Yes. I sent the check to Steve,' Alexander said.

"When did you get possession of the dog?" I asked.

"Steve sent his wife to deliver the dog to my house," Alexander said. "I got involved with some other buyers, so I sent Penelope to Steve's to deliver the check," Alexander said.

Penelope interrupted. "I've had enough of this. I'm leaving."

Alexander laid a hand on her arm. "Wait just a minute, Penelope. I have a question. "Did you deliver a check for $9,000 to Steve when you picked up Pepe?"

Penelope bowed her head and spoke softly, "I didn't deliver the check."

(During a moment of dead silence while her admission sank in, I noticed the auburn hair of this lady in the expensive green suit. *She probably has a temper to go with that red hair*, I thought.)

"I don't understand," Alexander exclaimed. "Why not? If you didn't deliver the check, what did you do with it?"

Penelope looked up. "Have you forgotten? We had a big fight. Instead of taking the check to Steve, I phoned him to tell him to come and get it if he wanted it. Steve wasn't there. His wife answered the phone. She said she would come and get the check. I told her I was going to Fort Worth and wouldn't wait for her. We agreed to meet at a half way point, at a Denny's Restaurant parking lot."

The conversation now had Paul's complete attention. "What about the check for $9,000? Did you give it to Steve's wife?"

"No," Penelope said. "I was so mad at Alexander, I didn't care. I thought I'd never see him again. I waited on Steve's wife for ten minutes. During that time I got to thinking about how the $9,000 would almost empty our bank account. The more I thought about it, the madder I got. I tore the check up into little pieces and started to leave. I saw Steve's wife drive up. She asked for the check. I made up a story about the sale being cancelled and that Alexander would pay a stud fee instead."

Alexander looked like a man who had just been slapped in the face.

"I'm sorry to have caused so much trouble," Penelope said. "At that point I didn't care if Alexander's business went down the drain. I thought I'd never see him again."

"Remember confidentiality," Paul said with his eyes fixed on mine.

"I remember," I said.

Then, to Alexander, Paul said, "Remember that everything said in here is confidential. The Mediator can't tell the other side about this unless you give him permission."

"What this angry woman did caused this whole mess, and cost all this time and money," Alexander said.

"Just watch your mouth," Penelope said, and started a list of Alexander's transgressions that she said was the real cause. Her voice grew louder with each word.

I held up both hands as if in surrender. "Wait, please. You two can settle that later. You don't need to take this mediation session's time for that." I lowered my hands. "Now, can we please get back to the business at hand?"

"Paul, do you mean we could just let this go as it is, fail to settle in mediation, and go to trial and keep our mouths shut about what Penelope said?" Alexander asked.

"You could. It's your choice," Paul answered.

"That's not right. I couldn't do it," Alexander said.

"Sure you can. Just keep your mouth shut," Penelope said.

"What should I do, Paul?

All eyes bore down on Paul.

"My advice, as your attorney, is 'tell the truth.' Give the Mediator permission to tell the other side what he learned, and let's get this thing settled," Paul said.

Back in the small room, I found Steve with his feet on the table again, the white baseball cap over his eyes and a soft snore on his lips.

"That was a long trip. Can we go home now?" Darrell asked.

I explained briefly what Penelope had confessed. "Now let me explain how I understand this case."

     (1) Steve made an oral agreement to sell Pepe to Alexander for $9,000.

     (2) Alexander accepted the offer, and promised to pay Steve the $9,000 price.

(3) Alexander delegated his wife, Penelope, to deliver the check to Steve.

(4) Penelope was angry at Alexander and declined to do as he asked. Instead, she phoned Steve's house to get Steve to come and get the check. Steve wasn't there.

(5) Steve's wife answered the phone, and volunteered to go pick up the check.

(6) Penelope was angry at her husband, and fearing that the $9,000 check would drain their bank account, she tore it up.

(6) Penelope made up a story about Pepe being on loan for stud service.

(7) When Steve's wife got home she repeated the story about Pepe being on loan for stud service.

I explained that Alexander and his attorney wanted the truth out in the open so they had asked me to explain the details of what they had just then learned.

Steve and Darrell returned to the large conference room and took seats across from Alexander and Paul.

Steve pulled his phone out of his pocket and called his wife at home. "You need to come down here," he said.

Without a word, Penelope walked out of the conference room. Through the large windows, all eyes followed her auburn hair as it reflected the sunlight. She hurried to her car and drove away.

Attention passed to Steve, who snapped his cell phone shut with a click. "My wife refuses to come," Steve said.

With the new revelations, the parties found it easy to reach a settlement agreement that included stud fees, to be paid to Steve and the return of Pepe. Alexander would keep the puppies sired during the two years he had possession of Pepe. Half the next litter sired by Pepe with Steve's female would go to Alexander. The attorneys agreed that there had been a contract, but that it had been mutually breached, so each party paid their own attorney fees.

The next day as I wrote my report to the court, and letters to the attorneys congratulating them on a job well done in negotiations. I wondered if Steve's wife was another red-head, but I dared not ask.

I also recalled what both Alexander and Steve had told me privately. There is something about the dog business that makes marriage difficult. Certain resources, physical, and emotional, seem to go to the dogs rather than the wives.

I. What is Mediation?

A Simple Explanation

A Mediator is a go-between, someone who helps two parties in dispute reach an agreement. A Mediator is necessarily neutral, and cannot take sides. The Mediator is sometimes referred to as neutral third party.

The Mediator is not a judge. He/she cannot give legal advice. The Mediator's goal is not to have a winner and a loser, but to have two winners. In a meeting where confidentiality is the rule, the Mediator helps the disputants reach an equitable settlement agreement.

Who is Who, and What is What?

Attorney: Legal counsel, licensed by the state, who represents the Plaintiff or Defendant.

Caucus: A private meeting of any two or more people involved in a mediation.

Cause: Another name for a court case, a cause of action. A cause is "styled" with the name of the Plaintiff and Defendant: Somebody vs Somebody-else.

Defendant: The person against whom the suit is brought.

Et al: Short for "and others."

Initiator: Person who brings a complaint against another outside a court of law that calls for mediation. The Initiator is equivalent to the Plaintiff.

Judge: The final decider in cases that go to trial.

Lawyer: Another name for an attorney.

Litigation: Action in court regarding a lawsuit. A lawyer who practices law in a courtroom is called a litigator.

Movant: One who asks the court to enforce or change a previous ruling. Like the Plaintiff, the Movant initiates legal action. For example a divorcee's former spouse fails to live up to a provision in the divorce decree. The divorcee makes a motion to the court to enforce the previous ruling in the divorce decree. Having moved, the person is a Movant.

Party: A Plaintiff, Initiator, Defendant, or Respondent. They are all parties to the conflict. A corporation or other entity can initiate a lawsuit or action that requires mediation. In that case the corporation is a party.

Plaintiff: The person who brings a lawsuit against someone else. Literally, "one who pleads." The Plaintiff is pleading with the court for relief. The Plaintiff is also synonymous with "accuser." Usually in his petition to the court, he/she accuses the Defendant of wrongdoing.

Pro bono: Work done without charge.

Pro se: The Plaintiff or Defendant in a lawsuit who represents himself without the aid of an attorney.

Respondent: Person against whom the complaint is made. He/she is equivalent of a Defendant.

Some Terms Associated

With Business Cases

Breach of Contract: One or more parties break an agreement, or fail to do as agreed.

Contract: An agreement between two people or entities to do certain things.

Debt: Something one person owes another.

Debtor: A person or entity to whom something is owed.

Some Terms Associated

With Family Cases

Custodial Parent: The parent who decides where the child will live.

Noncustodial Parent: The parent without the right to decide where the child lives.

Presumed Father: A husband of the mother when the child was born.

Modification: A change in a divorce decree regarding child custody, child support, visitation, relocation, etc.

Purpose of Mediation

Mediation is for the benefit of all concerned in a lawsuit. Mediation saves time and money for the Plaintiff, Defendant, and the Court. Mediators are not nearly as expensive as a trial. When you settle in mediation, you know exactly where you stand. If you go to trial, you never know exactly how it will turn out. Juries are like voters and footballs; you never know which way they'll bounce. Judges are human, and no two are exactly alike.

A great benefit of mediation is that both sides have an opportunity to have their say, unhampered by courtroom procedure. No one will say, "Just answer the question, yes or no," as might happen in a courtroom. Often when a person explains all the circumstances of a dispute, the other side begins to understand and it is a step toward a settlement agreement.

In cases where both parties have lawyers, attorneys for both parties and the Mediator agree on a date for mediation. In some cases one side has an attorney and the other doesn't. A Plaintiff or Defendant representing himself is called pro se. He/she too must agree on the time and date of the mediation.

If lawsuits could be frozen together in a lump, they would look like an iceberg. Only 10 % to 15 % would show on the surface. Most of the ice would be submerged and invisible. The small visible portion would be representative of the number of lawsuits that actually go to trial in a courtroom. The rest, 85 %, and sometimes 90 % of lawsuits filed in large city courts such as Dallas, never go to trial. If it were not for mediation there wouldn't be enough courthouses and judges for our litigious society.

Most large cities have hundreds of mediators. Many are attorneys who practice law and also serve as mediators. Some professional mediators have retired from other professions. For example, this writer, Joe B. Hewitt, is a retired pastor. Hundreds of other mediators are volunteers, whose only reward is the satisfaction of helping people.

One of the most successful mediation firms is Ken Burdin Mediations of Dallas. Burdin himself is not an attorney, but hires attorneys as mediators. He is an excellent mediator, but most of his work is in administration and marketing. "I'm a businessman," he said.

Mediation is a service given by altruistic people who want to help those who can't afford to pay a Mediator. Mediation is a profession, practiced by trained men and women for whom it is a livelihood. Mediation is a business, a service provided for profit.

Which of the above categories your Mediator fits depends on the nature and size of your case. Family conflicts, such as divorce, child custody and child support disputes involving people who cannot afford an attorney or a mediator will be done by a community organization of volunteer mediators. Most metropolitan areas have such organizations that also serve the needs of people involved in civil lawsuits who can't afford legal counsel or a professional mediator. However, much of the volunteer mediation work done is by professional mediators. Some is done by newly-trained mediators doing their practicum, a required number of mediations done before being credentialed.

I volunteer to do mediations through such an organization administered by Dallas County's Alternative Dispute Resolution Department. I also do *pro bono* mediations for destitute defendants in cases that courts have appointed me to mediate.

Some of the Dallas mediators have been involved in establishing the Texas Mediators Credentialing Association (TMCA). It was in a formative stage in 2002 when I started mediating, and I was among the first to register for credentialing.

All mediators who are credentialed by the TMCA are required to do a certain amount of *pro bono* mediations each year. They also must meet requirements in education, continued training, and ethics. Many states require that mediators be licensed. Since Texas' mediators do their own policing and discipline through TMCA, the State of Texas has not found it necessary to license mediators.

Mediation in the Court System

Courts use mediators to prevent overload in the court systems and to save litigants time and money. Mediators help settle all kinds of civil cases. A majority are contract disputes and bad debts. Vehicle accidents involving personal injury cases are numerous. There are so many divorce cases that in larger cities certain courts specialize only in family cases. Family court judges send cases to mediation where child custody, property settlement, and modification of previous court orders are settled.

Example Credit Card Case

Credit cards are easy to get. In years past, credit card companies mailed out cards to customers who had never asked for them. There are many ways you can get into credit card trouble, and I have seen them all in mediations.

A family of four uses credit cards as a convenience, but pays them off every month. Suddenly, the husband, the main income producer, becomes ill and can't work. His wife continues to work but pays only the minimum payment on the credit cards each month. The husband is totally disabled or dies. She continues using the cards, and gets further behind each month. Then another disaster strikes. Her car's motor burns up. She loses time at work. She buys another car so she can go to work and quits paying on the credit cards.

Interest and late charges pile up. Phone calls from collectors become more frequent, and finally she gets a letter from an attorney. He represents some company she never heard of and is threatening to sue if she doesn't pay on the debt. She learns that her credit card company gave up and wrote off her debt, and then sold her account, along with hundreds of others, to a collection company. She can't pay. He sues.

The case goes to mediation. She can't pay a lawyer, so she represents herself in the mediation session. The contested amount is less than $10,000, so she pays the minimum mediation fee. She is employed and has an income, so she does not qualify for free legal and mediation service from a charitable organization.

Ordinarily the Plaintiff Attorney will demand the entire amount, including interest, late frees, filing costs, and attorney fees. However, if she can borrow some money from Uncle Charlie, the bank, or from another credit card, he will take 80 % in full settlement.

She didn't get into trouble because she was stupid. She could not have avoided her husband's problems. So she won't do something stupid now like borrowing on another credit card and paying 24 to 29 % interest in order to pay off this one. However, she knows she owes the money, and wants to do what is right, so she offers to pay it off at $50 a month if the Plaintiff can reduce the amount down to just the principle, and without all the extra charges, and without adding any interest.

The Plaintiff won't consider such a small payment, but the offer is a beginning. He started high; she started low. The Mediator puts them in separate rooms and goes back and forth, urging her up, and urging him down.

This goes on for two or three hours. The Mediator tells the Plaintiff Attorney how hard the poor woman has had to live in recent years, of her children's illnesses and school expenses, necessary home maintenance and her own health problems. Then the mediator tells the woman that the attorney has a strong case and might prevail, getting everything he asks in court. Finally she calculates the most she can pay monthly, and he calculates the least he can take.

He makes his "last and final offer." If she raises her offer, he will usually listen, and might make the "last and final offer," two or three times later.

Eventually, they agree on a payment plan. The attorney insists that the pay-out be backed up with an agreed judgment. The Defendant must sign the agreed judgment, which will be filed with the court and used to seize any property she has that is not exempt if she defaults on the payments. As long as she makes her payments, the agreed judgment is dormant. When she makes her final payment, it goes away.

After the parties agree on the settlement, the attorney writes by hand the provisions on a form furnished by the mediator. Copies are made of the signed document. Then the attorney later draws up the final document and sends it to the other party for signatures. The hand written document is binding, and also serves to be sure the final document has not changed any of the provisions of the settlement.

You Have to Stick Up for Yourself

Circumstances and participants are disguised to preserve confidentiality.

Suzie has three maxed out credit cards, with balances ranging from $800 to $8,000. The largest, one I'll simply call a Blue Card, sued for the $8,000 balance plus $3,000 late charges, and $2,500 legal fees. Suzie is *pro se* and had never been in mediation previously. She received the court's Special Mediation Order and the rules for mediation, but she never read them.

The Blue credit card company had written off her debt and sold it to a collector for a few cents on the dollar. The collector waited until a week before the statute of limitations expired and filed suit, using a large law firm that specializes in debt collection that I'll call Winger and Wang. I negotiated with Suzie and the law firm for three months before we agreed on a mediation date.

A mediator cannot give legal advice. It is sad to see a *pro se* defendant come to mediation totally unprepared and ignorant of her rights. My advice is: Get a lawyer, and if you can't do that, at least read the Special Mediation Order,

Rules for Mediation, and my instructions on how to prepare.

Lou Wang, the Plaintiff attorney, asked during a telephone call, "Will the other side have any objection if our client does not fly here from South Dakota to the mediation? He will give me full authority to settle, and will be available by telephone."

"I don't know. I'll ask," I replied.

Here was a lawyer who wanted to do everything properly and obey the order that requires both parties to be physically present in the mediation session, but only if he had to. If the other side would give permission, his client could save the air fare, hotel, and other expenses involved.

I phoned Suzie and asked the question. It made no difference to her. No doubt, if she had an attorney, he would not have been so kind.

I sat at the end of the long conference table. Lou Wang sat on my left, and Suzie on my right. After all the preliminary explanation of the process, Lou presented his case. Suzie had used the credit card for ten years and quit paying on it. She owed $13,500. If she could pay a lump sum, he could reduce the payoff by 20 %. She could pay $10,800 cash and be done with it.

Suzie looked dumfounded. "If I had that kind of money, I wouldn't be in this mess." She sat in silence.

Lou told her how that he had everything in order to go to the court and ask for a Summary Judgment, that the court would surely grant it, and she would have to pay it as well as post-judgment interest, and her credit would be ruined.

Seeing the poor woman in an almost catatonic state, I took her into the caucus room. By asking questions away from the demanding attorney, Suzie began to relax and told me she owed the money and wanted to pay but could not. Still, she had difficulty sticking up for herself. She sat quietly.

I explained to her that I could not plead her case. She would have to do it herself, but I could certainly ask questions. More questions brought out the fact that her husband had died after a long illness during which she was his full-time caretaker. Her only income was his social security checks. The credit card bills had been incurred before he fell ill. When the family income stopped, she stopped paying.

In the big conference room Lou listened as I repeated what Suzie had told me. He phoned his client in South Dakota and received approval for a long payout. Eventually, after several trips between the conference room and caucus room, Suzie agreed to a monthly payment with no interest that would cover only the $8,000 balance, with payments to start in 30 days well after she started a new job.

In my opinion, Suzie could have done much better if she had stuck up for herself more, and if she had read the rules.

Why the Song and Dance?

Why didn't the attorney simply make his best offer in the
beginning, and why didn't the woman make her best offer
at the beginning, and settle the case in 15 minutes?
Mediations rarely work that way. Most usually the *song
and dance* of negotiations is necessary for each party to get
their best advantage. It's almost a required ritual. Although
it seems to some of us to be a waste of time, the best and
most equitable settlements result in the tried and tested
negotiation to settlement in mediation.

Personal Insults

Debt collectors make frequent use of the term *dead beat*. A
dead beat runs up bills with no intention of paying them.
Regardless of which side you are negotiating, it is
important that you not demean the other party. To suggest
the other party is a dead beat enflames conflict and makes
agreement more difficult. I had suspicions regarding a
divorce case I mediated. The couple had 27 credit cards
ranging from $800 to $8,000 debt on each one. How they
conducted their business was not the issue. Confidentiality
is one of the major foundation stones of mediation.
Courtesy is also important. If a negotiator resorts to
personal insult, he is demonstrating the fact that he has run
out of logical argument. The worst response to personal
insult would be to hurl another insult back.

Legal Loopholes

I have had lots of brilliant, original ideas, or so I thought. When I was in the eighth grade, I designed an automatic pistol that used recoil power to eject a spent shell and insert a new cartridge. I was quite excited until I found out that a better automatic pistol had been invented more than 50 years earlier. If you think that you have discovered something new and exciting about your case that is sure to make you a winner in court, be careful.

Many times a *pro se* defendant comes into the mediation room excited. He has found a law or case history that might magically get rid of the debt without him having to pay it. So if you are a layperson, thinking you have found loopholes or some rare escape route via legal maneuvering, think again. You may find that somebody else thought of that fifty years ago and changed the law or the procedure.

Still, you should study the documents involved.

The collector usually is alert to the statue of limitations and will file a week or a day before it expires.

Consumers are supposedly protected from usury, exorbitant interest rates. However, each state has its own definition of usury. For example, credit card companies might be incorporated in South Dakota for good business reasons, including being allowed to charge 29 % interest in addition to late fees.

Extenuating Circumstances Make a Difference

If there are legitimate, believable reasons why you got into financial trouble, the creditor will usually make you a better settlement offer if you can explain and document them.

Sometimes It's Better Not To Settle

(A mediator shouldn't say that.) For example, Jose borrowed money from a loan shark who charged him 20 % interest per month. Jose continued getting farther behind, and finally quit paying. The loan shark sued for the principle plus the exorbitant interest. In mediation, Jose offered to pay the principle only. The shark demanded more.

Apparently the shark's lawyer knew little about the case before he came to mediation. He told the shark he could not charge that kind of interest, and suggested that he settle, leaving off most of the interest. The shark argued with him and insisted he had all the interest coming. My duty as mediator was not to see to it that Jose was not taken advantage of. My duty was to the court, to try to get the case settled. The end result of the mediation was that both parties stood their ground. I finally declared an impasse. So the case went to trial, where I have no doubt that the judge punished the loan shark, and probably let Jose off without paying anything.

When it's best to Walk Away

The most contentious cases I have dealt with were appeals from JP Court to County Court. The parties had been fighting over a relatively small amount of money for two or more years. Bitter words were added to threats and insults. Both parties would be much better off just to call it quits by signing a settlement agreement giving nothing and taking nothing.

When it's best just to listen

Angry people need to vent. They want to express hurt and disappointment. I mediated a landlord/tenant case in which the landlord and I sat silently while the tenant expressed frustration because of what she perceived as ill treatment.

The monetary settlement was small and insignificant compared to the most important letter of apology. Not only was the lawsuit settled, but a friendship was restored.

Sometimes it's best to lose gracefully

A middle age woman had lost her husband to cancer. She had a $10,000 credit card bill that she could not pay. She was the only care giver for her aged bed-ridden mother. Her only income was $700 monthly Social Security for herself, and $700 for her mother.

She owed the money. She wanted to pay, but found no way. The Plaintiff Attorney suggested a monthly pay-out at $150 for five and a half years. She refused to consider it. She barely had enough money for food, and not nearly enough for medicine.

He told her what he thought would happen in court: the Judge would give the credit card company a judgment for $10,000 and possibly more.

The debtor could see two results of not settling the case in mediation. Either she would say "no" to a settlement and try to forget about it, and learn later that a judgment had been rendered by default. Or, she could go to court and try to convince the judge to award a judgment of a lesser amount.

I suggested that rather than do either of those, that she sign an agreed judgment, and get the case over with immediately as far as she was concerned.

I asked the Plaintiff Attorney if he would be willing to settle for the agreed judgment. He would. As the three of us gathered around the conference table, the Plaintiff Attorney explained to the Defendant that he would not try to attach anything she had that was exempt, such as her house and car.

"If I don't have anything, how can I have something that's not exempt?" she asked.

70 Per Cent Satisfied

An unscientific survey found that 70 % of people were satisfied with their settlement in mediation while 90 % who went to trial were not satisfied with the decision of the judge or jury in civil cases.

Typical Sequence of Events:

1. The Plaintiff files a lawsuit and sends a copy of the **original petition** to the Defendant so he will know what he is accused of and what the Plaintiff is asking the court to do.

A petition is a plea to the court for action to compel someone else to do something. The petitioner literally prays to the court for relief. For example,

> *Johnny borrowed my car and wrecked it. I'm pleading for the court to order Johnny to pay for my car repair and for my rental car, signed, Frankie.*

2. The Defendant **answers** the accusations in the Plaintiff's petition, and files the answer with the court. For example.

> *I, Johnny, deny all that, demand proof, and ask the court to dismiss the case and make Frankie pay all the court costs.*

3. The judge sets a **trial date** and appoints a **mediator.**

4. The Mediator contacts both the Plaintiff and the Defendant and arranges a date and time for the mediation. If they have lawyers, all communication is directed to the lawyers. If the parties can't agree on a mediation date, the mediator sets the date.

5. Each party attends the mediation with full authority to settle and pays an equal share of the mediator's fee. When the mediation is scheduled, the mediator usually asks for a small scheduling fee. Then when the parties appear for the mediation, they pay the balance of the mediation fee. If the case is settled prior to mediation, the case is dropped, somebody dies, or anything else happens that prevents the mediation from taking place, the scheduling fee becomes an administration fee to pay the mediator for the time he has spent on the case.

6. At the mediation, usually held in conference rooms in the mediator's office or other central location, the Plaintiff and his attorney sit on one side of the table. The Defendant and his attorney sit on the other side. The Mediator sits at the end. The Mediator suggests that the proceedings be informal, and that first names be used. He explains that everything in the mediation is confidential, that nothing that is discovered in the mediation can be used in court

later, and the mediator cannot be called to testify. No stenographic record or recording is allowed. Both parties are to understand the confidentiality rules. Nothing that is said or done in the mediation session is to be repeated elsewhere. The judge does not want to know what is said in mediation, only that the case was settled or not settled. Everyone is free to speak their mind without fear of future recrimination.

> *For example, Johnny confesses in mediation that he was dead drunk on the day Frankie's car was wrecked, so he doesn't know if he wrecked it or not. If the case doesn't settle in mediation, Frankie can't mention that revelation in court. The Mediator heard what was said. Neither party can call the mediator as a witness in court later.*

The only things exempt from the confidentiality rules are child abuse and elder abuse. The mediator, and anyone else learning of such abuse, is required to report it to the proper authorities.

7. Each side has uninterrupted time to present his/her case, and does so.

> A. The Plaintiff begins by stating his position and demands.

>> *Example: Frankie's attorney shows pictures of the damages on the car, reiterates the allegations in the petition and demands*

*$19,000 actual damages, and $2,000
attorney fees. He then produces an affidavit
from Johnny's sister that states she was in
the car with him when he wrecked it.*

B. The Defendant states his position and/or
demands.

*Example: Johnny says he could possibly
have wrecked Frankie's car, but he's not
sure. He can't remember. Johnny's attorney
offers $5,000 for complete settlement.*

C. The mediator reiterates these positions to make
sure he understands what each party is saying, and
that each party understands what the other is saying.

8. Both parties are asked to suggest possible terms of
settlement. These are negotiated back and forth until a
settlement agreement is reached.

*Johnny does not admit to any wrongdoing, but is
willing to pay $19,000 for the actual damages.
Frankie doesn't believe that is enough, but is willing
to take it. It wouldn't be worth the next $2,000 to go
to trial and possibly pay another $10,000 legal fees.
So Frankie settles, considering the $2,000 loss as
nuisance money.*

9. When both parties agree on the settlement, one of the parties, or his attorney, writes up the agreement, and the parties sign it.

The Caucus

Often one party wants to confer with the mediator in private. They go into another room for a caucus. Other caucuses might be between a party and his lawyer in private. The lawyers might want to caucus in private without the parties and mediator. Any combination of parties, attorneys, and/or mediator might caucus.

Sometimes when there are bad feelings between the Plaintiff and Defendant, the mediator will separate them right after the preliminary meeting, putting each party in a different room. Then the mediator confers privately with each party and conveys its offer of settlement to the other. If a settlement is not reached because of a lack of information or documents, the mediator may recess the mediation and reconvene at a later time.

If there is an impasse, and no settlement is reached, the mediator may stay in contact with the parties and try to get them to settle right up to the trial date. I have settled cases weeks or months after the parties gave up in a mediation session.

Whose Side Are You On?

When you go to mediation, remember that it is give and take. It is a venue for negotiation, and you have to stick up for yourself. It's best to have an attorney who will stick up for you, but ultimately the responsibility is yours. Most likely your lawyer won't drop the ball, but if he does, you had better scoop it up and run with it.

The mediator will be present to see that the proper process is followed and that you are not bullied or mistreated. Negotiation is up to you and your lawyer. If you are *pro se*, alone without a lawyer, all the responsibility for looking out for you is *yours*.

Mediation in Business and Industry

Mediation is also used in disputes where no lawsuit is involved. Business and industry are urged by mediators to mediate, don't litigate. A customer who believes himself to have been wronged by a company can agree with the company on a mediator and settle the matter without a lawsuit. Contract disputes between companies or individuals can likewise be mediated rather than going through the courts. The Better Business Bureau uses mediation extensively.

Pre-litigation Mediation

Parties in mediations where no lawsuit is involved, or pre-litigation mediations, are called the Initiator (the one who starts the action) and the Respondent, rather than Plaintiff and Defendant.

Pre-termination Mediation

Business and industry are also urged to mediate, don't terminate. A valued employee with a grievance can be kept on the job if differences between the employee and a supervisor can be mediated and settled to the satisfaction of both. Human resources disputes, and labor disputes often can be settled in mediation and be the beginning of a long term cordial relationship between employee and employer. The United States Postal Service and other governmental entities use mediation extensively.

Develop Negotiating Skills

If you are a party or attorney in a mediation you are there to get the best settlement you can. While the mediator is busy being neutral and trying to help both sides, you should be seeking your own best interests.

It is advisable to hone up your negotiating skills. If you play chess, you have an advantage, because you have learned to plan several moves ahead, anticipate moves by your opponent, feint moves, sacrifice moves, and ambush. If you haven't learned to play chess it would sharpen your negotiating skills if you would learn.

In addition to standard courses in negotiation, I recommend the 2000-year-old book, *The Art of War* by the Chinese military genius Sun Tzu.

My colleague, Irene Zucker, President of Verbacom Executive Development, teaches negotiation to small groups of executives or one-on-one. If you are about to be involved in high-dollar negotiations, a tutor is a good investment.

Don't Let a Master Lawyer

Intimidate You

The case involved a young restaurateur I'll call Sylvester, who was sued by Albert, owner of the Acey-Deucy Remodeling Company. Names and pertinent facts have been changed to preserve confidentiality.

A grease fire broke out in Sylvester's restaurant kitchen and caused extensive smoke damage to the building's interior. Firemen sprayed water to put out the fire, leaving black walls, and an inch of water on the floor. Sylvester called Acey-Deucy for an estimate to clean up and repair the damage.

Albert, owner of Acey-Deucy, told Sylvester that he would have to hire an outside service company to take out the two inches of water on the floor, and tear out the soaked carpet and carpet pad. Then Acey-Deucy would replace the faulty vents, tear out and replace the blackened sheet rock, paint the interior, and install new carpet.

Albert handed Sylvester a contract for the work that called for payment of $31,000 when the work was done,

"I put in a call to my insurance company. They're sending out an adjuster on Monday," Sylvester said. "I hope I don't have to wait until then to get the job started."

Albert assured Sylvester that he could start the job immediately and have it finished by Monday.

"I'd like to be sure the insurance company will pay the bill," Sylvester said. "I'm down to nothing in operating capital. The only way I can pay is through the insurance." He gave the insurance policy to Albert, who handed it to his assistant, Jane.

Albert instructed his assistant to carefully read the fine print and be sure Sylvester's fire damage was covered. "If you see anything that might cause them to deny coverage, text me immediately."

Albert hired extra manpower, and worked around the clock for two days. Monday morning Sylvester entered the restaurant with an insurance adjuster in a heated argument.

The grease fire was not covered by insurance.

Like other disasters, events leading up to this one were unexpected and in rare combination. Jane got into a fight with her boyfriend and neglected to read the policy. Sylvester's partner from whom he had split six months earlier, had promised to take care of an insurance inspector's complaint of grease buildup in the vents over the grills. Since the insurance company's warnings had been ignored, the insurance coverage for the grease fire was nullified.

Sylvester didn't pay Albert. Albert had exhausted his own operating capital to finish the job, and was more than sore at Sylvester. Sylvester was mad at his ex-partner and the insurance company, but was too broke to hire a lawyer.

Albert filed suit *pro se* against Sylvester asking for $31,000 actual damages, and another $20,000 for damage to his reputation and business. The court ordered the case to mediation.

Sylvester arrived early for mediation, and took a seat to my left in the conference room. Albert, his business partner, and another man came in and sat across the table from Sylvester.

After the preliminary instruction about the mediation process, I asked The Plaintiff, Sylvester, to present his position. He briefly explained what had happened, and showed the contract Sylvester had signed.

Sylvester then explained that he had no money when the fire broke out. He had told Albert that he could not pay, and that Albert took on the project gambling that the insurance company would pay. So, as much as Sylvester regretted it, Albert had gambled and lost. Sylvester didn't owe him anything.

The third man with Albert spoke up. "I will prevail in trial. There is no doubt. . ."

Who is this guy? I wondered. Albert had introduced him by first name like he had introduced his business partner. Sylvester had expected to be negotiating with another layman, like himself, but Albert had brought an attorney. This one had likely read *The Art of War*; He had the element of surprise, and superior forces.

Then the lawyer continued: "Not only will we get a judgment for the $51,000, but you will also have to pay attorney's fees because it is a breach of contract case. In addition to that I will run up your cost to go to trial by about $8,000 or $10,000. There will be depositions and other expenses." The lawyer continued on for several minutes while Sylvester seemed to shrink down in his chair.

Sylvester protested that he had no money. He was barely able to stay in business. His partner had disappeared along with all their cash. He felt terrible about Albert's loss, but was helpless to do anything about it.

"I think it's time for us to divide up. I'll take Sylvester into the other room. . ." I began.

"Just a minute, sir," the lawyer interrupted. "I think we can work this out to everyone's satisfaction." His tone had changed from combative to conciliatory. "Your business, Sylvester, is worth about $150,000. You still owe $50,000.

Your handshake partner who left you in the lurch, is no longer in the picture. You need a partner who can pull his weight."

Sylvester's countenance perked up.

"Any idea about who would make a good partner?" The lawyer continued. "Maybe someone you have known for a long time, who has already put most of the money he had into your business?"

"You mean Albert?"

The lawyer had a document with him that spelled out the partnership arrangement in detail. Sylvester was delighted to sign it and have Albert as a partner.

This settlement was equitable, I believed. However, you as a party in mediation, should be alert for a master lawyer who might not have a fair settlement in mind.

Unrealistic Expectations

The following is a composite of several cases using fictitious names.

Tyrone's car was rear-ended by Patricia, who was driving her father-in-law's car. At the accident scene, an exit ramp off an Interstate Highway, Patricia became emotional, cried, and ran to Tyrone's car to see him lying down in the front seat of his car moaning. She declared that the accident was all her fault and called 911. She told Tyrone that she had good insurance and that his loss would be well covered.

Patricia's husband and father-in-law arrived just as paramedics were lifting Tyrone out of his car and into an ambulance. Her father-in-law inspected his car and found no damage. Her husband inspected Tyrone's car and found the paint on his rear bumper to be scarred.

In the hospital emergency room, Tyrone complained of back and neck pain and was given several expensive tests, which came back negative. Tyrone continued to complain of back and neck pain and went to a chiropractor and then to a pain management physician.

Tyrone hired an experienced attorney who filed suit against Patricia, and her father-in-law asking for a $1 million to cover $30,000 in medical bills, that included $6,000 for chiropractor fees, and pain and suffering. Patricia's insurance company had already paid $2,000 to put a new rear bumper on Tyrone's car. The Court ordered the case to mediation. Patricia's insurance adjuster and attorney, her father-in-law's insurance company's adjuster and attorney, and Tyrone and his attorney, appeared for mediation.

After the preliminary speech by the mediator, explaining confidentiality, and his neutrality, Tyrone's attorney presented his case and demanded $1 million.

Patricia's insurance company attorney expressed sympathy for Tyrone's suffering, and agreed that his insured was at fault in the accident, but took exception to the great amount of medical costs incurred in view of the minor damage caused by the accident. He had already offered Tyrone $800 to settle the claim.

The mediator ushered Tyrone and his attorney into another room where Tyrone told how his back and neck hurt constantly and had been since the accident.

Back in the conference room with the two insurance company lawyers, the mediator heard how that Tyrone had made a personal injury claim on the average of one a year for the past nine years, always claiming permanent damage to his back and neck. If Tyrone got a settlement for only the medical costs, the $30,000 in medical costs would be discounted 60 % or more, which Tyrone and his lawyer would pocket, one of the lawyers said. "So they're shooting for $1 million, and hoping for $18,000 net."

The gap between $1 million demanded and $800 offered, is a definite challenge for a mediator. He must not judge. He must not take sides. But he can ask questions and warn of peril. And a trial is usually perilous. Settlement in mediation is a sure thing. A trial is "iffy." The mediator especially emphasized this to Tyrone and his attorney.

Offers and counteroffers continued for three hours until Tyrone demanded the medical costs of $30,000. The Defense offered $1,500, saying, "This is a nuisance offer to end the case. We have no doubt that we would prevail in court. But we are willing to pay a token to end it and avoid the expense of a trial."

At that point both sides refused to budge. The mediator asked permission of both sides to make a mediator's proposal. They agreed. The mediator wrote a proposed settlement amount of $5,000. The insurance company adjusters said, "No way." Tyrone's attorney said he should take it. Tyrone said, "No way."

Tyrone had gone into the lawsuit with unrealistic expectations. He may have been one of those people who mistakenly equate accident with getting rich. His lawyer tried during the mediation to bring Tyrone down to earth and take something in mediation rather than almost certainly to get nothing in a trial and take a risk of having to pay the Defendants' attorney fees.

The mediator declared an impasse, and notified the court that no settlement had been reached in mediation. For the next six months the mediator stayed in touch with both parties. Tyrone's attorney was allowed to withdraw from representing him because Tyrone would not return his calls or correspondence. Tyrone did not appear for trial, and the court ruled for the Defendants.

This was an extreme example of unrealistic expectations. Tyrone's lawyer represented him on contingency. If he didn't win, the lawyer got nothing and Tyrone got nothing. I doubt that Tyrone's lawyer investigated Tyrone's past, otherwise he probably would not have taken Tyrone's case. So Tyrone's lawyer turned out to be the big loser.

Another example of unrealistic expectations: Two women, old friends, had a falling-out over a debt. Each was convinced that she was right and would prevail in court.

Neither had an attorney. The Plaintiff filed first in small claims court, claiming that she had loaned the Defendant $1,000, which she refused to repay. The Justice of the Peace court ruled in favor of the Plaintiff and awarded her $1,000 judgment.

The Defendant posted bond and appealed to County Court. The County Court Judge wisely referred the case to mediation.

The Plaintiff's position: "I loaned her $1,000. She didn't pay. She owes me."

The Defendant's position: "She gave me $1,000 to pay for my wedding. During the wedding reception she got mad at me, and demanded that I pay her back. I don't owe her anything. She owes me for insulting and stalking me constantly for the past three years. My husband left me to get away from her constant harassment."

Not having an attorney to bring them down to earth was a problem left to the mediator. Each woman had her mind set. Neither would consider any kind of compromise with the other. Although I had them in separate rooms, and each woman had family members with her who tried to calm her, each steadfastly promised to fight on "until justice is done."

I recognized that it wasn't the money that was stuck in these women's craws, but something else deep seated now and covered up. Something had happened in the wedding reception that opened an old wound, experienced a profound rejection, or exposed a deep embarrassment. Neither woman, however, would consider such a possibility but railed on about the money.

Whatever the real cause of the animosity between the former friends, expecting $1,000 given, or received, to fix the problem, was an unrealistic expectation. If your heart was broken, you might not want to admit it, but rather trade in the emotional hurt for a financial one, and convince yourself that $1,000 would sufficiently punish the one who broke your heart and make you feel better. The transference to $1,000 could have been profound embarrassment caused by the other person. Money wouldn't fix that either, but it would be less embarrassing to fuss about.

While each of the contentious women were in separate conference rooms, and I went back and forth between them, I tried to convince each one to "walk away." They had both already spent more than $2,000 on the case. I urged them to "Stop the bleeding" by signing a settlement agreement that stated that each party would pay nothing and take nothing and would take no further action, commonly known as "walk away."

Each woman's family members with her urged her to "walk away" and be done with the conflict. Their minds, however, were set and locked into position. They fought on, repeating the same argument over and over. Family members with them were exhausted and insisted they give it up and go home. Both contentious women refused. Finally I gave up and called an impasse.

The Principle of the Thing

I have mediated many cases in which the principle of the thing turned into deal breaker. "It's not the money; it's the principle of the thing," sounds very honorable, but can be very costly. For example: You've been sued. The Plaintiff is a jerk. His case is really full of holes. You go to mediation and negotiate with him. Finally, he says he will settle for $1,000. You know he's wrong. If you pay the money, justice will not be served, so you decide to fight because of the principle of the thing. You spend $10,000 fighting him, and finally prevail in court, but the court doesn't award your attorney fees. It's contrary to the American ideal of fair play, but you'd be $9,000 better off to have paid the $1,000 nuisance money. Facing reality isn't always the most ideal, but it usually is the cheapest.

In some cases a mindset proved to stop a settlement. A young woman was being sued for a large debt. She appeared *pro se*. The Plaintiff attorney made a good offer of settlement with long terms. She couldn't make a decision. Her mind was in neutral.

Finally, after a half day of negotiations, with her mouth zipped shut most of the time, I declared an impasse and we all went home. I gave her a couple of days to think about it and phoned her, urging her to consider the settlement offer.

She wouldn't make a decision. I suggested she hire a lawyer just for consultation. It wouldn't be too expensive just to get him to recommend a decision for her own best interest. She wouldn't make that decision either. I called her several times over a period of three weeks as the trial date approached. She finally quit answering the phone, apparently recognizing my number on caller ID. Later I checked with the court to see how her case came out. She lost big. Not long afterward, unable to continue making her house payments, she lost her home.

Just plain emotional attachment to a cause can so clutter up a person's mind that he can't face reality. Your absolute, ironclad conviction, "it's the principle of the thing," won't transfer to a judge or jury.

In a contract dispute, a wife told me with trembling chin what a great man her husband was, how he loved people, and how he was kind to people. However, no matter how kind he was, as far as the opposing party was concerned, none of that would change the facts about whether he did or did not sign a contract.

I don't mean to say, "Leave your emotions at home." Real, heartfelt emotions often pave the way for an equitable settlement. Just don't depend on your emotions to serve in place of hard facts.

I have been pleasantly surprised to see jaded attorneys for debt collectors, who have heard it all, go out of their way to help a debtor who has been injured and unable to work.

Come to Mediation Prepared

A typical exchange of unprepared people is: "You say you paid the bill. Do you have a receipt or cancelled check?"

"Yes, somewhere."

Another one is: "Are you sure my client made those charges? Do you have some documentation?"

"Oh, yes. The bank has all that."

The other side would be much more convinced if you could show them the cancelled checks or charge slips.

In another case a *pro se* Defendant said, "I don't know why I'm here. I got the notice from the mediator, so here I am, but I don't know what it's about." He was too busy, I suppose, to look at his mail, or to read the notice handed to him by a process server that said, "You have been sued."

The poor guy was at a disadvantage because the other side did know what was going on and came prepared.

It is advisable to have a lawyer with you at mediation. If you don't have a lawyer, take someone with you, a business associate who knows something about the case, your wife, husband, or friend.

If You Forget About It, It Won't Go Away

No matter how many millions of times it has been proved wrong, some people still believe, "Just forget about it and it will go away." It doesn't go away. It just gets bigger, meaner, stickier, and more costly. If you are notified that you are to appear in a mediation, get your documents, and your thoughts together, and show up on time. If a party fails to appear, I wait 45 minutes. If they don't show up or call, I try to reach them by telephone. If I can't, and they don't call to say they're on their way, I declare them a "No-Show" and notify the judge.

If you fail to appear at a court-ordered mediation, the court's order says you will be subject to sanctions. Judges don't like to have their orders disobeyed.

There Is No Remedy At Law

For Every Wrong

The United States has long had a reputation for being a litigious society. We seem to others to always be ready to sue at the slightest provocation. We also are sensitive to fair play and justice. We want justice to be done. We expect justice to be done. Neither a new law nor a lawsuit will right every wrong.

A great proportion of lawsuits end up with the instigator wishing he never started it. It costs money to hire a lawyer and pay court costs

Prepare To Be Lied To

Part of your preparation for mediation involves the expectation that you might be lied to. The vast majority of lawyers and parties to lawsuits with whom I have mediated are honest and will tell the truth. However, you never know when you will be negotiating with one of the few who will lie.

My wife, Marona Posey, often issues a warning that came from many years of law practice: "People lie." She is more cynical about it than I, but regardless of the proportion of liars, the person going into mediation needs to be prepared to face people who lie.

Because of the confidentiality rule, you can't depend on the mediator to get the truth out of an opposition party. Here is an example case:

Two partners, Benjamin and George, were sued by a supplier, I'll call Samuel. The Defendants did not deny that they owed him money. However, they disputed the amount owed, and told Samuel they were broke anyway, and couldn't pay anything. (No confidence is broken by this example, which is sufficiently disguised that no one could ever identify the people involved.)

During the opening session, I asked the business partners, "Have you been in mediation before?"

"No," each man said.

Before I could begin my explanation, their attorney spoke up. "Listen, this is a waste of time. These guys have no money and no prospects for the future. They can't pay anything, let alone what the Plaintiff is demanding."

Having heard words to that effect many times, which nearly always turn out to be incorrect, I did not respond, but continued with my opening remarks. I explained the mediation process, my neutrality, the strict confidentiality, and my determination to help the parties settle the case.

The Plaintiff attorney laid out the signed contract, copies of invoices, past due notices, and demand letters. The Defense attorney agreed that the Partners owed money, but argued that the charges had been exorbitant. Because they had overpaid for their merchandise they had to raise their prices. People quit buying, and the Partners, Benjamin and George, went deeply into debt just to stay in business. The financial disaster was all the Plaintiff's fault for overcharging, the attorney said.

I took the Partners Benjamin and George and their attorney into a caucus room and asked, "What do you want to see done here today?"

"I know we owe the guy, but we're broke," said Benjamin, the younger partner, who did all the talking with the exception of a grunt now and then from George, the older, larger partner.

"These guys can't pay anything. They're judgment proof," the attorney said.

"What does that mean? The judge won't give him a judgement?" Benjamin asked.

"It means you don't have anything they can attach if they get a judgment. They can't touch your home, your car, or the tools of your trade," the attorney answered.

"So, if he gets a judgment, he just gets a piece of paper."

"So, you want Samuel to write off the debt and forget about it?" I asked.

"That would be nice, but I hesitate to put it that way," the attorney said. "They need to nonsuit the case because there is no point in going to trial. I'll demand a jury trial. I'll subpoena expert witnesses. Even if Samuel prevails in court, it will cost him upwards of $20,000 to try the case. Then if he gets a judgment, it will be worthless."

I reasoned with them about the benefit for all concerned if the case could be settled and over with, and urged them to make an offer, no matter how small. The Defense attorney continued to say "No."

Back in the other room, Samuel and his attorney looked expectant. "What did they offer?" Samuel asked.

"Nothing. They say they're broke."

"I know better than that," Samuel said. "George is pretty broke, but Benjamin isn't," the Plaintiff attorney said. "George has a gambling habit and stays broke. Benjamin, however, has property other than his homestead, some undeveloped land and some rental property." He asked that I tell Benjamin about his findings. Perhaps Benjamin would begin negotiating with some kind of offer.

Laughter from the caucus room greeted me as I entered. Benjamin laughed and said, "I can't decide between Oklahoma and Louisiana."

"You can leave your money there just as easily as Las Vegas," his lawyer said.

George spoke for the first time, "What goes to Vegas stays in Vegas. I've left a lot of money in casinos in all three states. You better stay away, Benjamin."

"Samuel's attorney told me some things that you need to know," I said.

The happy faces faded away.

"What's that?" Benjamin asked.

"He said that you have several pieces of rental property that could be seized in a judgment.

The Partners' attorney said, "May we have a few minutes?"

"Sure." I left the room. A half hour later, the door opened, and the attorney motioned for me to come back in. I don't know what was said during the 30 minutes I was gone, but I can guess that Benjamin and George's attorney had a talk with them about how the ground of deception can be as dangerous as quicksand.

"If Samuel will reduce his demand from $30,000 down to $15,000, we'll offer to pay it off in monthly installments of $50," the attorney said.

I knew what Samuel's reaction would be, that it was a ridiculous offer. Still, I recognized what it really was, a beginning in negotiation.

I went back and forth from one room to the other with offers and counter offers. Through questioning I pointed out weaknesses and strengths trying to get Benjamin to increase his offer and trying to get Samuel to lower his demand.

The confidentiality rule did not allow me to tell Samuel about Benjamin's plan to go to the casinos and gamble the next weekend or to say he had been lying about being broke.

During the negotiations, Samuel admitted that on a few of the invoices an employee had charged well over the market price for his goods. "That's neither here, nor there," he said, and quoted an old saying. "Let the buyer beware."

Finally Benjamin offered $5,000 down and $500 a month until $25,000 had been paid. Samuel said no to the offer and that he couldn't afford to "donate" $5,000 to Benjamin and George. "Tell them I'll take $25,000 cash, however."

"That's a lot of money for someone to come up with who's broke," his lawyer said.

After several more trips between the caucus rooms, they settled for $22,500 cash, payable in 90 days.

I had not believed the Partners to be broke, but I partially believed it or I would not have been so surprised at the cash amount. My wife was correct, "People lie. It's one of life's realities. In mediation and all other negotiations, we have to accept the fact and work around it.

 I wouldn't say that Benjamin's attorney lied. He repeated what Benjamin and George had told him. That didn't make him a liar. However, his bluster and posturing had the same effect, and was something else to ignore or work around.

The Finesse

Negotiators use a wide variety of ploys. Here is an example:

It's a high-dollar contract dispute that has been ordered to mediation by the court. The mediator's fee will be high. The attorneys negotiate back and forth several times during the weeks leading up to the scheduled mediation. Their offers are far apart.

One week before the scheduled mediation, the Defense notifies the Plaintiff, "Our offer will be zero, and won't change. Therefore, we see no use in going to mediation and should cancel."

The Plaintiff protests that mediation should proceed. The mediator insists that no party can unilaterally cancel mediation even though the other party refuses to appear.

The Defense decides to save the mediation fee by not appearing, since the Plaintiff obviously will not appear.

On the appointed mediation day, the mediator appears, and the Plaintiff appears. The Defense does not. The mediator reported to the Court that the Defense did not appear. The Court sanctioned the Defense. The Defense pled, "The

Plaintiff told us he would not appear, so we didn't either."
The claim that the Defense had been deceived made no
difference to the judge.

"Not so," Claims the Plaintiff. "We took to heart the
mediator's admonition and changed our mind, thereby
complying with the court's order, which the Defense
ignored." The Plaintiff has "finessed" the Defense.

In another case the Defense did not respond to the
mediator's requests to negotiate a mediation date. Letters,
phone calls, faxes, emails, are not answered. None are
returned, so the mediator assumes that the party has been
served, knows about the mediation and is receiving the
communications.

"Is he going to show up?" asks the Plaintiff.

"Probably not," said the mediator.

"I see no reason to go to the conference room if he's not
going to appear," says the Plaintiff. The mediator agrees
and sends a letter to the Defendant stating that since he has
not responded, the mediator considers it a refusal to
mediate and he will report it as such to the Court and cancel
the mediation session.

On the appointed day the Defendant appears in an empty
conference room and reports to the Court that neither the
other side nor the mediator appeared. What about the letter
notifying him mediation was cancelled? What letter?

Mediator's Proposal

A Last Ditch Effort at Settlement

If you have been in a mediation session several hours and everyone is tired, the parties are close together on a dollar amount, but won't budge, it may seem that the case won't settle. However, there is one tool, not often used, that might work, called the Mediator's Proposal.

Here is a typical example:
"Look, we started out asking $100,000, and now we have come down to $39,750, which is far below what we think we could get in court, but we just want to get it over with. It's our final offer. If you can't accept it, then let's go home," the Plaintiff said in a voice of exasperation.

The mediator scribbled a note, got up, opened the door, turned and said. "I'll convey this offer to the other side. They already said they wouldn't pay a dime over $35,000, but maybe they'll up it some."

As the door closed the Plaintiff attorney calls out to the mediator, "He'd better come up to the $39,750."

The mediator knocked on the door of the other conference room. Inside he found the Defendant and his attorney busy packing to leave.

"They're stuck on $39,750," the mediator said.

"That's what they were stuck on before. Do you mean they didn't come down at all?," the Defense Attorney said as he stuffed documents into a black leather briefcase.

"Yes, that's right."

"Well, we've yielded all we can. It was like squeezing every drop to be able to offer $38,000," the Defendant said. "I'm ready to go home."

"Just a minute. There is one thing we might do," the mediator said.

"What's that, give them a pound of flesh?" the Defendant asked.

"Let me give a mediator's proposal."

Both men stopped packing and sat down at the conference table.

"It might work," the Defense attorney said.

"Maybe. It all depends," the Defendant said.

"Do you want to do it?" the Defense Attorney asked his client.

The Defendant thought a moment, scratched his head, and said, "Okay. Let's give it a try."

The mediator hurried back to the other conference room to see the Plaintiff and his lawyer
packing documents. "I have a mediator's proposal,"

"They won't budge, and we won't budge, so what's the use," the Plaintiff said.

"Let's at least look at it," the Plaintiff attorney said.

His client agreed. The mediator sat down and wrote by hand, "Defendant pays Plaintiff the following, $30,000 today, $8,000, in 30 days, and an additional $1,050 in 60 days." He left the note with the Plaintiff and his attorney, and then returned to the Defendant and attorney. The mediator wrote the identical terms on a piece of paper and slid it across the table to the Defendant. The mediator's proposal required an answer within 24 hours.

Both parties accepted the mediator's proposal, and the case was settled.

In another case where only $1500 separated the two tired parties after a half day's mediation, my mediator's proposal would have taken one party to only $500 from his demand.

He adamantly refused, however. His exasperated attorney volunteered to cut his fee $500.

Check in the Mail

A Move of Desperation, Better Than Surrender

When at an impasse, and one party has offered a cash settlement and the other party has refused to accept it, if you are willing to do an act of desperation, here's one that works about half of the time:

Able has sued Baker for $10,000. Baker's final offer after two hours of negotiating was $5,500. Able came down to $6,250, but wouldn't go any lower. The mediator put the mediation in recess and Able left. Baker packed up and started out the conference room door.

"Wait just a minute," the mediator said. "I have an idea."

"Okay," Baker said without enthusiasm.

"Get a cashier's check to Able for $5,700, with a notation 'in full settlement,' and put it in the mail with a signed settlement agreement."

When Able, three days later, had had time to mull over the failed mediation, opened an envelope and held a check for nearly what he had demanded, he couldn't resist depositing the check and signing the settlement agreement.

How to Prepare for Mediation

Working With Your Lawyer

Need for a Lawyer:

Getting sued, that is, being the Defendant, is bad news. It costs money, time and trouble. If you, as the Plaintiff, sue someone, it costs you money, time and trouble. There is no way to avoid it. Usually the best money either Plaintiff or Defendant can spend is for a good lawyer.

Other than in small claims court (Justice of the Peace Court), no one should file a lawsuit without a lawyer any more than he/she would go to surgery without a doctor.

Your lawyer is your champion. He/she will fight for you. But you have to give your lawyer all the needed information. Don't expect your lawyer to always know what to ask for. It's better to offer too much information than not enough. It's better to bring too many documents to a mediation session than not enough. To say, "Oh the bank has that on record," is not nearly as convincing as handing someone a cancelled check with their signature on it. Often a party will make a statement about an invoice or contract, but can't produce the document. If you hope to have all your ducks in a row, give your attorney all the documents he might possibly need or bring them to the mediation session yourself. It is not unusual for an attorney to bring in a box of documents on a wheeled cart.

Many times one party will make a statement of fact. The other party says, "Show me." If the allegation can be backed up with a document, you're on your way to settling the dispute.

Face Reality

One of the impediments to settlement in mediation is when
a person has listened to so many easy money stories and
boasting lawyer ads that he loses touch with reality. A
Plaintiff, emotionally involved, spills out his story to his
attorney. It's a chinch to be a winner, the Plaintiff
convinces the lawyer. The lawyer, having heard only one
side of the story, tells the Plaintiff to expect a big
settlement or court judgment.

The Plaintiff goes into mediation all pumped up and
expecting great things. During the mediation things are
brought up that he hadn't realized earlier. The other guy
does have a leg to stand on. The Plaintiff's lawyer
recognizes that the case is not locked up after all and tries
to convince his client to settle for less.

If you're that Plaintiff, you must fight your way through
emotion and a wounded sense of justice, and force yourself
to face reality. Your lawyer hasn't turned on you; it's just
easier for him to change gears when the road ahead
suddenly goes uphill, because he has had more experience.

Caution. Follow the Money

Old friend and international entrepreneur Mike Jones, says if you want to learn the true motivation in a labyrinth of confusion, "Follow the money."

If you are the Plaintiff in a lawsuit, an attorney may paint a beautiful picture of your pockets stuffed with money, especially if you are paying a sizable retainer fee. If you have difficulty understanding why he urges you not to settle, "follow the money." Who will profit, and who will lose? The percentage of lawyers that would take advantage of you are very small, still, some will encourage you to refuse to settle in mediation and go to trial knowing they don't have a strong case. You'll pay your attorney fees whether you win or lose. Whereas, if you settle in mediation, the attorney fees stop accruing.

I must emphasize that the vast majority of attorneys are honest and ethical. I have dealt with hundreds of attorneys, and the number of those of questionable ethics and real "jerks" could be counted on one hand.

However, you should be alert. Look out for your own best interests. Most likely your attorney is looking out for you, but in some circumstances, consider the possibility that he is looking out for himself first.

Be Alert for the Unexpected

Unknown factors come out in mediation that were not previously known. For example, in Tyrone's case, when his previous claims of personal injury and multiple accidents involving back and neck injuries came to light in mediation, it changed the entire picture. Tyrone's lawyer immediately knew he had no case, and tried to bring Tyrone down to reality.

In another personal injury case the Plaintiff claimed back and neck injuries and demanded payment for a future lifetime of pain and suffering. In mediation the Defendant, who admitted culpability in the accident said, "I suffered the same impact as he did. I wasn't hurt at all, and I'm 74-years-old." That new information changed everything. The Plaintiff attorney had to convince his client to reduce his expectations and demands drastically, and the case was settled.

How to Find a Mediator

The Internet is a good way to find mediators. You will find them listed in several organizations. Asscciation for Conflict Resolution (ACR), is a national organization of mediators, www.acresolution.org. ACR also has regional chapters. The Texas Association of Mediators (TAM), www.txmediator.org. The Texas Mediator Credentialing Association, www.txmca.org, has a list of mediators who have met the organization's standards of experience, ethics, and training.

Rules for Mediation

The following are Texas rules, which will agree with most other states.

Definition of mediation. Mediation is a process under which an impartial person, the mediator, facilitates communication between parties to promote reconciliation, settlement or understanding among them. The mediator may suggest ways of resolving the dispute, but may not impose his own judgment on the issues for that of the parties.

Conditions precedent to serving as mediator. The Mediator shall not serve as a mediator in any dispute in which he has any financial or personal interest in the result of the mediation. Prior to accepting an appointment, the mediator shall disclose any circumstance likely to create a presumption of bias or prevent a prompt meeting with the parties.

Authority of mediator. The Mediator does not have the authority to decide any issue for the parties, but will attempt to facilitate the voluntary resolution of the dispute by the parties. The Mediator is authorized to conduct a joint and separate meeting with the parties and to offer suggestions to assist the parties achieve settlement. If necessary, the mediator may also obtain expert advice concerning technical aspects of the dispute, provided that the parties agree and assume the expenses of obtaining such advice. Arrangements for obtaining such advice shall be made by the mediator or the parties, as the mediator shall determine.

Parties responsible for negotiating their own settlement. The parties understand that the mediator will not and cannot impose a settlement in their case. The mediator, as an advocate for settlement, will use every effort to facilitate the negotiations of the parties. The mediator does not warrant or represent that settlement will result from the mediation process.

Authority of representatives. Party representatives must have authority to settle and all persons necessary to the decision to settle shall be present. The names and addresses of such persons shall be communicated in writing to all parties and the mediator.

Time and place of mediation. The mediator shall fix the time of each mediation session. The mediation shall be held at the office of the mediator, or at any other convenient location agreeable to the mediator and the parties, as the mediator shall determine.

Identification of matters in dispute. Prior to the first scheduled mediation session, each party shall provide the mediator and all attorneys of record with an information sheet and request for mediation on the form provided by the mediator setting forth its position with regard to the issues that need to be resolved. At or before the first session, the parties will be expected to produce all information reasonably required for the mediator to understand the issues presented. The Mediator may require any party to supplement such information.

Privacy. Mediation sessions are private. The parties and their representatives may attend mediation sessions. Other persons may attend only with the permission of the parties and with the consent of the mediator.

Confidentiality. Confidential information disclosed to a mediator by the parties or by witnesses in the course of the mediation shall not be divulged by the mediator. All records, reports or other documents received by a mediator while serving in that capacity shall be confidential. The Mediator shall not be compelled to divulge such records or to testify in regard to the mediation in any adversary proceeding or judicial forum. Any party that violates this order shall pay all reasonable fees and expenses of the mediator and the other parties, including reasonable attorneys fees, incurred in opposing the efforts to compel testimony or records from the mediator.

No stenographic record. There shall be no stenographic record of the mediation process and no person shall tape record any portion of the mediation session.

No service of process at or near the site of the mediation. No subpoenas, summons, complaints, citations, writs or other process may be served upon any person at or near the site of any mediation session upon any person entering, attending or leaving the session.

Termination of the mediation. The mediation shall be terminated: a) by the execution of a settlement agreement by the parties; b) by declaration of the mediator to the effect that further efforts at the mediation are no longer worthwhile; or c) after the completion of one full mediation session, by a written declaration of a party or parties to the effect that the mediation proceedings are terminated.

Interpretation and application of rules. The Mediator shall interpret and apply these rules.

Fees and expenses. The Mediator's daily fee, if agreed upon prior to mediation, shall be paid in advance of each mediation day. The expenses of witnesses for either side shall be paid by the parties producing such witnesses. All other expenses of the mediation, including fees and expenses of the mediator, and the expenses of any witness and the cost of any proofs or expert advice produced at the direct request of the mediator, shall be borne equally by the parties unless they agree otherwise.

About the Author

Author Joe B. Hewitt started writing as a newspaper reporter for the Lima, Ohio, News. He covered the police beat, courthouse beat, and was an investigative reporter. He went under cover for three months and published an expose of vice and crime. He served as national and international news editor and "slot" man on the city desk.

He owned and published Texas weekly newspapers, Throckmorton Tribune, and Springtown Review, and was a stockholder, editor and publisher of the Richardson Digest while a student in seminary.

His newspaper career ended when he was called into the ministry. While still a seminary student he started the Richardson East Baptist Church, Richardson, Texas. By the time he graduated from seminary his new church had bought land on Main Street and built a building.

During the first several years at that church he worked as public relations director for a church-supported temperance organization. In that capacity he wrote teacher in-service training manuals on drug abuse, designed catalogs, edited a monthly magazine, wrote and voiced public service radio announcements, and appeared on television interview shows regarding drug abuse education, and spoke at high school assemblies and churches.

He enlisted others to voice public service announcements including Steve Allen and Dale Evans. He turned down an offer to become associate executive director of the organization and pastored the church full time.

During the 13 years at the Richardson church, he ghost-wrote a book on Bible prophecy for a famous radio preacher.

He resigned that pastorate to go into vocational evangelism. However, during those four years he was called by Christian leaders in many communities to lead special election campaigns. Of 13 major campaigns, he won 11. He turned down an offer to manage a US Congressman's re-election campaign.

Feeling a need to get back into the pastorate and following a desire to move to Rockwall County, Texas, he accepted a call to Pastor First Baptist Church of Fate, Texas, where he served 13 years. He built a home on 7.5 acres in rural Rockwall County.

He then became founding pastor of Princeton Park Baptist Church, Rowlett, Texas, where he served 9 years and retired in 2001.

During those years in the pastorate he wrote a nonfiction book on personal experience that has sold 45,000 copies. He wrote curriculum for Bible study teachers and teachers' commentaries for LifeWay, the publishing arm of the Southern Baptist Convention, as well as the youth devotional guide, and Open Windows the 1.1 million-circulation adult devotional guide. For 10 years wrote columns for the Rockwall Success, and Rowlett Lakeshore Times, local newspapers. His magazine articles were published in Mature Living, The Baptist Standard, and Leadership magazine (published by the Baptist General Convention of Texas), Faith for the Family, Reproduction Methods, and the Christian Crusader. Photographs have been published by Associated Press, United Press International, Popular Mechanics, and several detective magazines (from the days when he was police reporter.).

His travel articles and pictures have been published in The Dallas Morning News, and the Houston Chronicle's Sunday Magazine. Guest editorials have been published in The Dallas Morning News and Spirit of 76, publication of Fort Worth, Texas, Mensa.

Hewitt was certified by North American Mission Board, Southern Baptist Convention, as expert on Cults. He conducted seminars and workshops on Cults, Jehovah's Witnesses, Mormonism. Islam, Marriage Enrichment, Conflict Resolution, and Parenting. Hewitt is registered as an expert witness on Jehovah's Witnesses and testifies in child custody cases.

Hewitt served as a temporary missionary in Mexico, Brazil, Russia, Oregon, Idaho, New York, and pastored a church in England for a month in an exchange with the pastor of the English church. He served as volunteer chaplain and coordinator of jail ministries for the Rockwall County

Sheriff's Department for 10 years. He also served two days a month as volunteer chaplain at Lake Pointe Medical Center in Rowlett for 10 years.

On one of his three trips to Russia, Hewitt preached in Muravlenko, Siberia, a city of 40,000, built on 600 feet deep permafrost located 1,650 miles east-northeast of Moscow. The nearest airport was 100 miles south at Nyabresk where the Aeroflot plane broke down and Hewitt and his wife were stranded two days.

In addition to the mission trips, Hewitt visited Cypress, Turkey, Lebanon, Syria, Israel, Greece, Italy, France, Spain, Colombia, Panama, Costa Rica, and many Caribbean islands. Hewitt has traveled extensively throughout all 50 of the United States, Mexico and Canada.

After retiring from the pastorate in 2001, Hewitt began training as a mediator and has served Dallas and area courts as a court-appointed mediator to settle lawsuits. He was trained in general mediation, family law, Child Protective Services mediation, restorative justice, and arbitration. Although he has had experience in many kinds of mediation, his practice in recent years has been mostly in contract disputes, personal injury vehicle accidents, and general business disputes.

He is a member of First Baptist Church, Rockwall, Texas, Texas Association of Mediators, and Mensa, the high IQ society. He is rated by the Texas Mediators Credentialing Association as a Distinguished Credentialed Mediator.

Hewitt received a BD degree from Bible Baptist Seminary, and an MA degree in Biblical Studies from Dallas Baptist University.

Hewitt's wife of more than 50 years, Mary Louise "Marilu" Covert Hewitt, died in 2001. In 2003 Joe married Marona Posey, a retired attorney, novelist, a fellow Mensan, and partner in Hewitt and Hewitt Mediators.

Other Books by Joe B. Hewitt

Nonfiction

A Pastor's Adventures, the Good, the Bad, and the Sad.
Nonfiction, autobiography/memoir, 6x9, 228 Pages,
paperback or e-book. ISBN-13: 973-1499277098.

Trivia for Adults, 6X9, 150 Pages, and e-book, ISBN
13:978-148813419.

Rescatando a los Prisioneros de los Atalcya ,6X9 258
Pages and e-book, ISBN 978-1-48129-686-1.

Rescuing Slaves of the Watchtower, ISBN 978-1-61315-
006-1.) 6X9 Paperback, or e-book, 262 Pages.

I Was Raised a Jehovah's Witness, 4th Edition, Revised
and Updated 6X9 Paperback 224 Pages or e-book. ISBN-
13:978-1492909156.

Fiction

Murder on the Sky Ride, Mystery, 6X9, 300 Pages, ISBN
978 098 4989 706, paperback or e-book.

Mystery of the Vanished Gold, Mystery, 6X9, 236 Pages,
ISBN 13:9781491063705, Paperback or e-book.

My Love, My Enemy
Fiction/Historical, 6X9 Paperback 284 pages, or E-book,
ISBN 978-1494326029; LCCN 2014902417

All of this author's e-books are available wherever e-books
are sold. They are also available for loan from your public
library through Overdrive.

Links
Visit my website: http://www.joebhewitt.net
http://www.joebhewittmediator.com
Follow me on Linkedin:
https://www.linkedin.com/in/joebhewittmediator
Friend me on Facebook,
https://www.facebook.com/joe.b.hewitt
https://twitter.com/@joebhewitt

Contact Information

Joe B. Hewitt, PO Box 495711, Garland, Texas 75049-
5711.